PORTMANTEAUS AND MORE

PORTMANTEAUS AND MORE

Let's Have Some Fun With English

CHARLOTTE SMITH

Archway Publishing books may be ordered through booksellers or by contacting:

Archway Publishing
1663 Liberty Drive
Bloomington, IN 47403
www.archwaypublishing.com
844-669-3957

ISBN: 978-1-6657-3968-9 (sc)
ISBN: 978-1-6657-3969-6 (e)

Library of Congress Control Number: 2023904100

Print information available on the last page.

Archway Publishing rev. date: 03/21/2023

Dedicated to my grandsons Levi and August

CONTENTS

INTRODUCTION TO PORTMANTEAUS

A portmanteau (port-man-TOE) is a word that comes from the French and has a literal meaning and a figurative meaning. Literally, a portmanteau is a suitcase or trunk, usually made of leather and opening into two identical parts. Figuratively, a portmanteau is a word made from two (or more) other words. For example, one of the earliest portmanteaus is "smog," which is made up of smoke + fog. Just like you have to unpack a suitcase, you have to unpack a portmanteau word to see what two or more words form it. The two halves of the luggage fold into one piece. The parts of a portmanteau word fold into one word.

We are seeing more and more portmantcaus in every day life now, and most of them are a lot of fun. When possible, I have tried to educate the reader. Some of these portmanteaus you will know, some you will not know, and some you knew but just did not realize where they came from. I hope you enjoy these.

PORTMANTEAUS

A

Accenture = accent + (on the) future

Adidas = ADI (nickname of founder Adolf) + DASsler (his last name)

administrivia = administrative + trivia (dull things)

adorkable = adorable + dork

advertainment = advertising + entertainment

advertorial = advertisement + editorial

adware = advertising + software

affluenza = affluent + influenza: wealthy but without motivation

agiprop = agitation + propaganda (Russian)

aioli = ail (Fr. for garlic) + oli (Fr./L. for oil)

air-mageddon = air (travel) + Armageddon

Al-Anon = alcoholics + anonymous

Alcan = Alaska + Canada: 1,390-mile highway

Alcoa = aluminum + company + America

alcopop = alcohol + pop (as in soda pop)

Algol (computer language) = algorithmic + language

alliternation = alliteration + nation (examples: Russian roulette or Chinese checkers)

alliterockers = alliteration + rockers (examples: Beastie Boys, Foo
 Fighters, Sly Stone, etc.)

alnico = aluminum + nickel

alone = all + one (Middle English)

alphabet = alpha + beta (Latin)

alphanumeric = alphabetic + numeric

Americares = America + cares

Amerind / Amerindian = American + Indian

ampersand = and + per se + and (& = "and")

amphicar = amphibious + car (1961–1968)

Amtrak = American + track

Amway = American + way

anacronym = anachronism + acronym: a very old acronym that no
 one remembers, like BASIC

animagic = animated + magic

Animaltronics = animal + electronics: song

Animaniacs = animal + maniacs: cartoon

animatronics = animated + electronics

anticipointment = anticipation + disappointment

Antifa = anti + Fascist

appletini = apple + martini

aprium = apricot + plum: hybrid

aquaculture = aqua (water creatures) + agriculture

athleisure = athletic (clothes) + leisure (clothes), comfortable and
 appealing

Aussiedoodle = Australian shepherd + poodle

autobot = autonomous + robotic organism

autobus = automobile + bus

avionics = aviation + electronics

avocolada = avocado + piña colada

B

backronym = back acronym (example: "rap" is a backronym
of "rhythm and poetry" that also serves as a mnemonic
memory device)

Backsync = Backstreet (Boys) + NSYNC

bacne = back + acne

badjective = bad + adjective

badvertising = bad + advertising

baecation = bae (sweetheart) + vacation

balun = balanced + unbalanced: an electrical term

Bancorp = bank + corporation

barcade = bar + arcade

Barmageddon = bar (games) + Armageddon: television show

bash = bang + smash

bass (pronounced like base) = big + ass (all about that), song by
Meghan Trainor

Bassetoodle = Basset hound + poodle (NOTE: I have listed some
of the most popular poodle crossbreeds, but there are many
more!)

Batusi = Batman + watusi

beardo = beard + weirdo

Bearizona = bear + Arizona: wildlife park in Williams, AZ

beautimous = beautiful + fabulous

beefalo = beef + buffalo

beetabaga = beet + rutabaga

Belieber = believe + (Justin) Bieber: a fan

Bennifer = Ben (Affleck) + Jennifer (Lopez)

Benzo = Ben + Enzo (from TV's "The Challenge")

Bernco = Bernalillo (NM) + county

Bernedoodle = Bernese mountain dog + poodle

Beverly Hillbillies = Beverly Hills + hillbillies

bigkini = big + bikini

Billary = Bill (Clinton) + Hillary (Clinton)

biodrama = biographical + drama

bionic = biology + electronic

biopic = biographical + (motion) picture

Bisquick = biscuit + quick

bit = binary + digit

Blackula = Black + Dracula

blaxploitation = Black + exploitation

bleep = blank (out) + beep

blitzburgh = blitz + Pittsburgh (Steelers)

blog = weB + LOG

blotch = blot + botch

blurt = blow + spurt

boatel = boat + hotel

Bobo = bourgeois + Bohemian

bodacious = body (or bold) + audacious (which may mean bold or
        it could mean a little disrespectful)

boggle = boxer (or Boston terrier) + beagle

BoJo = Boris + Johnson: former Prime Minister of England

Bollywood = Bombay (in India, now called Mumbai) +
        Hollywood

boost = boom + hoist

botox = botulism + toxin

boxerdoodle = boxer + poodle

brainiac = brain + maniac

Brangelina = Brad (Pitt) + Angelina (Jolie)

brash = bold + rash

bratchos = bratwurst + nachos

BravoCon = Bravo (TV channel) + convention

breathalyzer = breath + analyzer

Brenaissance + Brendan (Fraser) + Renaissance

Brexit = Britain + exit (from EU, European Union)

Brisvegas = Brisbane (Australia) + Las Vegas (Nevada)

Britcom = British + comedy

broast = broil + roast

broccoflower = broccoli + cauliflower

brochacho = brother + muchacho

broga = bro + yoga

brogrammer = bro + programmer

Brojects = brothers + projects: television program

bromance = bro + romance: close, nonsexual friendship between
        two men

brond = brown + blond (hair)

brony = bro/brother + (My Little) Pony (fan); plural bronies

brotox = brother + botox

brunch = breakfast + lunch

buffeteria = buffet + cafeteria

bumble = bungle + stumble

C

cafetorium = cafeteria + auditorium

Calexico = California + Mexico: city in CA

Californication = California + fornication

cama = camel + llama

camcorder = camera + recorder

canimal = cannibal + animal

Canimals = can + animals: television show, animals in cans

cantini = can + martini

caplet = capsule + tablet

carjack = car + hijack

Casamigos = casa (Spanish for house) + amigos (Spanish for
        friends): tequila made by George Clooney et al (Latin for
        "and others")

cassingle = cassette + single

catio = cat + patio

cattalo = cattle + buffalo (bison)

caucacity = Caucasian + audacity

Cavapoo / Cavoodle = poodle + Cavalier King Charles spaniel

celebutant(e) = celebrity + debutant(e)

cellophane = cellulose + diaphane

Centcom / Cencom = central + command

Champa (Bay) = champions + Tampa (Bay)

cheeseburger = cheese (sandwich) + hamburger

Chiberia = Chicago + Siberia

chillax = chill + relax

Chiweenie/choxie = Chihuahua + dachshund

chocoholic = chocolate + alcoholic

chortle = chuckle + snort (first appeared in Lewis Carroll's poem
        "Jabberwocky")

Christmasketball = Christmas + basketball

Chug = Chihuahua + pug

chump = chunk + lump

Chunnel = channel + tunnel: connects England and France,
        underwater

cinemaholic = cinema + alcoholic

Cinemax = cinema + maximum

cineplex = cinema + complex

Cinnamoji (faces) = Cinnamon (Toast Crunch Cereal) + emoji

Cîroc = cime (Fr. for peak) + roche (Fr. for rock): vodka

Clamato = clam + tomato (juice)

clash = clap + crash

clasp = clutch + grasp

Claydies = Clayton + ladies ("The Bachelor")

cli-fi = climate + fiction: a sci-fi genre

Clorox = chlorine + (sodium) hydroxide

clump = chunk + lump

Coca-Cola = coca (leaves) + kola (nuts)

cocacolonization = Coca-Cola + colonization: globalized
    American culture

cockapoo = cocker (spaniel) + poodle

cockerdoodle = cocker (spaniel) + poodle

cojito = coconut + mojito

Cologuard = colon + guard

comcast = communication + broadcast

Comic-Con = comic (book) + convention

Comsat = communications + satellite

Conair = convict + airline: movie with Nicolas Cage

ConnecTV = connect + television: streaming services

contrail = condensation + trail (from an aircraft)

coopetition = cooperation + competition

copaganda = cop + propaganda

CoronaRita = Corona (beer) + margarita

cosplay = costume + play

Costco = cost + company

couchpotatriot = couch potato + patriot

(Count) Chocula = chocolate + Dracula: cereal

Covid = COrona VIrus + Disease

Coywolf = coyote + wolf

craisin = cranberry + raisin

cremains = cremated + remains

crimeminister = crime + (Prime) Minister

Crisco = crystallized + cottonseed (oil)

crit = critical + hit: a gaming term

crocubot = crocodile + robot (cartoon)

Croissan'wich = croissant + sandwich

cronut = croissant + donut

Crooklyn = crook + Brooklyn

Cruella de Vil = cruel + devil

crunchtada = crunchy + tostada (Taco Bell)

crunk = crazy + drunk (there are variations of this)

cruspy = crust + crispy

cyberbullying = cybernetic + bullying

cyberspace = cybernetic + space

cyberzine = cyberspace + magazine

cyborg = cybernetic + organism

cyngineered = cynically + engineered

D

dadication = dad + dedication

dadsplain = dad + explain

dadvice = dad + advice

daisy = day's + eye

dancercise = dance + exercise

Daniff = Great Dane + English mastiff

daycation = day + vacation

Desilu = Desi (Arnaz) + Lucille (Ball): a television production
    company

DHL (shipping) = (Adrian) Dalsey + (Larry) Hillblom + (Robert)
    Lynn

Dijonnaise = Dijon + mayonnaise

Dinomania = dinosaur + mania

DiscOasis = disco + oasis (Los Angeles, California)

Dixiecrat = Dixie + Democrat (1948)

Dobro (guitars) = Dopyera + brothers (also a word meaning
    "goodness" in their native Slovak)

docudrama = documentary + drama

docuseries = documentary + series

docusoap = documentary + soap (opera)

doga = dog + yoga

Dollywood = Dolly (Parton) + Hollywood

dopiary = dope + topiary (shaping shrubs or trees into objects)

dorf = dork + dwarf

dorgi = dachshund + (Welsh) corgi

dramedy = drama + comedy

druthers = I'd + rather

dumbfound = dumb + confound

dumpster = dump + Dempster (Brothers), inventors

dunch = dinner + lunch

dunt = dumb + c____

DWIsolation = DWI + isolation

E

ebike = electronic + bike

eblast = email + blast

ebonics = ebony + phonics

ebook = electronic + book

ecar = electric + car

ecard = electronic + card

ecase = electronic + case (in law); others are ecommerce, ebusiness, ebanking, esurance, elog

ecash = electronic + cash

echeck = electronic + check

ecigarette = electronic + cigarette

econometrics = economy + metrics: statistics

ecoteur = ecological + saboteur

ecrime = electronic + crime

ecycling = electronic + cycling

edate = electronic + date

edutainment = education + entertainment

eggflation = egg + inflation

eggstitute = egg + substitute

e-How = electronic + how-to (guide)

elearner = electronic + learner

electrocution = electricity + execution

email = electronic + mail

emopop = emotion + pop (music)

emorap = emotion + rap (music)

emoticon = emotion + icon

endorphin = endogenous (internal) + morphine

ensushiastic = enthusiastic + sushi (Grubhub)

envirotainer = environment + container

ereader = electronic + reader

erecycling = electronic (devices) + recycling

eruptiversary = eruption + anniversary (as in Mt. St. Helens, WA) escalator = escalade + elevator

eshopping = electronic + shopping

esign = electronic + signature

esport = electronic + sport

etail = electronic + retail

Eurafrican = European + African

Europol = European + police (office)

ewallet = electronic + wallet

ewaste = electronic + waste

ezine = electronic + magazine

F

Fabletics = fabulous + athletics: workout clothes (by Kate Hudson, et al)

fabulosity = fabulous + quality

faction = fact + fiction

fandelier = (ceiling) fan + chandelier

fantabulous = fantastic + fabulous

fantasnaek = fantastic + snack (Grubhub)

fanzine = fan + magazine

fauxhawk = faux + Mohawk: a popular haircut

fauxpology = faux (fake) + apology

favicon = favorite + icon

FedEx = Federal + Express

finsta = fake + Instagram

FinTech = financial + technology

fitacular = fit + spectacular (Planet Fitness)

flagel = flat + bagel

flare = flame + glare

flatform = flat + platform (shoe)

flaunt = flout + vaunt

flavorite = flavor + favorite

flexitarian = flexible + vegetarian

flispy = flavorful + crispy

flog = film + blog

flooreo = floor + oreo: five-second rule from the TV show
    "Ghosts"

flop = flap + drop

flounder = flounce + founder (or possibly blunder)

footvolley = football (soccer) + volleyball

fortnight = fourteen + nights

Fortran = formula + translation: computer language

framily = friends + family

Franglais = French + English

Frankenfood = Frankenstein + food: genetically-modified food

frappuccino = frappé + cappuccino

freecycling = free + recycling: giving away usable items

freegan = free + vegan

freeware = free + software

frenemy = friend + enemy

friendsgiving = friends + Thanksgiving

frings = (French) fries + (onion) rings

froffle = frozen + waffle

frogurt = frozen + yogurt

frosé = frozen + rosé (wine)

froyo = frozen + yogurt

frunk = front + trunk

fugly = f_____ + ugly

fummer = fall + summer: warm days in fall

funcle = fun + uncle

funderstruck = fun + thunderstruck

funfetti = fun + confetti

funkadelic = funky + psychedelic

funkind = fun + mankind: M & Ms

futurama = future + panorama

G

Gainiac = Gain (detergent) + maniac (a pun on a song from the
movie *Flashdance;* Gain detergent commercial)

galentine's (day) = gal + Valentine

galumph = gallop + jump / triumph (appeared in Lewis Carroll's
nonsense poem "Jabberwocky")

gasohol = gasoline + alcohol

gastropub = gastronomy + pub / public house: bar that sells food

gaydar = gay + radar

gaymer = gay + gamer

geep = goat + sheep

Gen Con = Geneva + Convention (this gaming convention
originated in Geneva)

genome = gene + chromosome

germinator = germ + terminator

gerrymander = (Eldridge) Gerry + salamander; Gerrymandering
is the practice of politicians' drawing of district lines that
favor their party; Gerry was governor of Massachusetts,
signer of Declaration of Independence, and the fifth
vice-president)

ginormous = gigantic + enormous

glamazon = glamor + Amazon: tall glamorous woman

glamma = glamor + gramma (grandma)

glamping = glamor + camping (RV)

gleek = Glee (TV show) + geek

glimmer = gleam + shimmer

glitterati = glitter + literati (fashionable, glamorous people)

glitz = glamor + ritz

glob = gob + blob (or possibly globe + blob)

globalquerque = global + Albuquerque (New Mexico): a
        celebration of world music and culture

glocal = global + local

glowdeo = glow + rodeo: part of world-famous, largest balloon
        festival, Albuquerque, New Mexico

goldendoodle = golden (retriever) + poodle

goodbye = God + be + ye

goon = gorilla + baboon

granfluencer = grandmother / grandfather + influencer

grapple = grape + apple

greige = grey + beige

grillbilly = grill + hillbilly

grocerant = grocery + restaurant

grolar bear = grizzly (bear) + polar (bear)

Groupon = group + coupon

grum = grim + glum

guesstimate = guess + estimate

gunfu = gun + kung fu (for example, in the John Wick movie
        franchise)

Gwake = Gwen (Stefani) + Blake (Shelton)

H

hangry = hungry + angry

Hasbro = Hasssenfeld + brothers: toy company

hassle = haggle + tussle

haterade = hater + Gatorade

hazmat = hazardous + material

heliport = helicopter + airport

herstory = her + history

historiography = history + biography

horgi = husky + corgi

humongous = huge + monstrous

HypochondriActor = hypochondriac + actor: a podcast

I

Ig Nobel (Award) = ignoble + Nobel

imagineer = imagine + engineer

impromedy = improvise + comedy

incel = involuntary + celibate / celibacy

Indigi-Genius = indigenous + genius: PBS television show

infomercial = information + commercial

Infosys = information + system (India)

infotainment = information + entertainment

Innoventions = innovation + invention: Epcot Center, Walt Disney
        World, Orlando, Florida

Instagram = instant camera + telegram

Instawork = instant + work

intercom = internal + communication

internaut = internet + astronaut: frequent user

Internet = international + network

Interpol = international + police

interrobang = interrogative + bang: a superimposed question mark
    and exclamation mark

Investco = investment + company

Invisalign = invisible + aligner (for teeth)

irresist-a-bowl = irresistible + bowl (Applebee's)

itchsanity = itch + insanity (from Cortisone commercial)

J

jackalope = jackrabbit + antelope

jamocha = java (which means coffee) + mocha (espresso /
    chocolate)

janties = jean + panties

Japanimation = Japan + animation

jarts = javelin + darts

jazzercise = jazz + exercise

jeepney = jeep + jitney: Philippines' public transportation,
    originally a five-cent jitney ride

jeggings = jean + leggings

Jeoparday = Jeopardy + day

JoBros = Jonas + Brothers

Jonagold = Jonathan + Golden Delicious: hybrid apple

jorts = jean + shorts

Josthansson = (Colin) Jost + (Scarlett) Johansson

J-pop = Japanese + pop music (out of Tokyo)

J-Rod = JLO (Jennifer Lopez) + Arod (Alex Rodriguez)

Juneteenth = June + nineteenth (first celebrated in 1865 in Texas to
    commemorate the freeing of slaves)

K

Kcal = kilo + calorie (1000 calories)

Keanaissance = Keanu (Reeves) + Renaissance

Kellyoke = Kelly (Clarkson) + karaoke

Kenergy = Ken (doll) + energy

Kete = Kim (Kardashian) + Pete (Davidson)

keytar = keyboard + guitar

kidvid = kid + video

Kimye = Kim (Kardashian) + Kanye (West)

kingdom = king + domain

Kotex = cotton (the k is for Kimberly-Clark) + texture

K-pop = (South) Korea + pop (music)

Kravis = Kourtney (Kardashian) + Travis (Barker)

L

Labradoodle = Labrador (retriever) + poodle

LasagnaMac = lasagna + macaroni and cheese (from Stouffer's)

laze = lava + haze

LEGO = leg + godt (Danish for "play well")

lesbytarian = lesbian + Presbyterian

liegasm = lie + orgasm (faked)

liger = lion + tiger

LiMu (emu) = Liberty + Mutual

linner = lunch + dinner

listicle = list + article: a piece of writing in the form of a list

lituation = literature + situation

lobsessed = lobster + obsessed (Red Lobster)

locavore = local + carnivore or herbivore or omnivore (one who
   eats only locally-grown food)

LoDo = LOwer + DOwntown (Denver, CO)

lox = liquid + oxygen

lum = lunar + module

lupper = lunch + supper

M

madVlad = mad + Vladimir (Putin)

maglev = magnetic + levitation: train

Mahomey = (Patrick) Mahomes + homey

malternative = malt + alternative

Maltipoo = Maltese + poodle

malware = malicious + software

manbag = man + handbag

manel = man + panel

manimal = man + animal

manny = male / man + nanny

manpanion = man + companion

manscape = man + landscape: shave private areas of the body

mansplain = man + explain

manual/mannual = man + annual (trip)

Manwich = man + sandwich

manx = man + Spanx

maser = microwave + laser

maskne = mask + acne

mathlete = math + athlete

Mcjob = McDonald's + job: unskilled, rather dead-end job

Mcmansion = McDonald's + mansion: mass-produced houses for
    the middle class

meatflation = meat + inflation

mechatronic = mechanics + electronic

Medevac / Medivac = medical + evacuation

Medicaid = medical + aid

Medicane = Mediterranean + hurricane

Medicare = medical + care

Megxit = Meghan + exit (refers to Meghan and Harry stepping
    away from royal duties)

meld = melt + weld

Menurkey = Menorah + turkey

meowgarita = Meow Wolf + margarita

metcon = metabolic + conditioning (Cross Fit)

methlete = methamphetamine + athlete

metrosexual = metropolitan + (hetero)sexual

Mexicali = Mexico + Calexico (California)

Mexicue = Mexican + barbecue

Michelada = mi (Spanish for my) + chela (Spanish slang for beer) +
    ada (short for Spanish helada meaning cold); a Mexican type
    of Bloody Mary

microvalve = microscale + valve

MiG (Russian) = (Artem) MIkoyan + (Mikhail) Gurevich:
    designers

mimsy = miserable + flimsy (appeared in Lewis Carroll's nonsense
    poem "Jabberwocky")

mobilegeddon = mobile + Armageddon: Google search engine
    algorithm

mobisode = mobile + episode

Mobituary = Mo (Rocca) + obituary: podcast about remarkable
    people

mockamole = mock + guacamole

mocktail = mock + cocktail (non-alcoholic)

mockumentary = mock + documentary

modem = modulator + demodulator

momager = mom + manager

momcation = mom + vacation

momfluencer = mom + influencer

momplicated = mom + complicated

mompreneur = mom + entrepreneur

momsplain = mom + explain (explain something to a childless
    person in a condescending way)

momster = mom + monster

Mopar = motor + parts (Company)

moped = motor + pedal

MoPo = Maury + Povich

Morkie = Maltese + Yorkshire terrier

motel = motor + hotel

motocross = motor + cross (country)

motorcade = motorcar + cavalcade

Motown = motor + town (Detroit, Michigan)

moval = modern-day + oval (diamond)

movember = moustache + November (event of growing a mustache
    in November for awareness of men's health issues)

multiplex = multiple + complex

multiverse = multiple + universe

Muppet = marionette + puppet

murse = man + purse

N

Nabisco = National + Biscuit + Company

nacation = naked + vacation

napalm = NAphthenic + PALMitic (acids)

Nar-Anon = narcotics + anonymous

Narluga = Narwhal + Beluga (whale)

neatnik = neat + beatnik

neek = nerd + geek

nerdtastic = nerd + fantastic

Nervive = nerve + revive

Nescafé = Nestlé + café

Nespresso = Nestlé + espresso

Nesquik = Nestlé + quick

netiquette = (inter)net + etiquette

netizen = (inter)net + citizen

netocracy = (inter)net + aristocracy

newscast = news + broadcast

NiCad (battery) = nickel + cadmium

NoDak = North + Dakota

nojito = no + mojito (mojito without alcohol)

NoLita = north (of) + Little Italy (NYC)

Nollywood = Nigeria + Hollywood

nomance = no + romance

nonsoon = no + monsoon

nope = no + dope (this may be questionable, but I like it!)

Nutrishop = nutrition + shop

Nutrisystem = nutrition + system

O

Obamacare = (President) Obama + (health) care

obsessionado = obsession + afficionado

onomatomania = onomatopoeia (a word that sounds like the actual
 sound it makes, for example, buzz, beep, hiss, boom) +
 mania

opart = optical + art

Ouija (Board) = oui (Fr. for yes) + ja (Ger. for yes)

Oxbridge = Oxford + Cambridge

Oxfam = Oxford + famine (Oxford, England, Committee for
 Famine Relief)

P

palimony = pal + alimony

Pan Am = pan (Greek for all) + American (originally Pan
 American Airways, later Pan American World Airways,
 now defunct)

PanCAN = pancreatic + cancer: organization fighting the disease

pand-emmys = pandemic + Emmys

Panera = pan (Latin for bread) + era (Latin for time)

paralympics = paraplegics + Olympics

paraski = parachute + ski

paratrooper = parachute + trooper

paratroops = parachute + troops

peacenik = peace + beatnik

Pekapoo = Pekingese + poodle

penultimatum = penultimate + ultimatum (final demand before an
 ultimatum)

PepsiCo = Pepsi + Company

phablet = phone + tablet

phenomaly = phenomenon + anomaly (an oddity)

phubbing = phone + snubbing

phygital = physical + digital: interactive technology

Pictionary = picture + dictionary

pilk = Pepsi + milk

Pinterest = pin (bookmark) + interest

pitsky = pitbull + husky

pixel = picture + element

pizzapreneur = pizza + entrepreneur (from "The Bachelor")

pizzly = polar (bear) + grizzly (bear)

pizzone = pizza + calzone

plandid = planned + candid (photo)

pleather = polyurethane + leather

plogging = (Swedish) plocka upp, "picking up litter" + jogging

plumcot = plum + apricot: hybrid

pluot = plum + apricot: hybrid

podcast = iPod + broadcast

Pokémon = pocket + monster

Pollywood = Punjabi / Pakistan / India + Hollywood

pomato = potato + tomato: tomato on the vine and potato in the
        same soil, grafted

poopetrator = (dog) poop + perpetrator

popsicle = pop + icicle

portmanteau = porter (Latin for carry) + manteau (French for coat)

positv = positive + tv: movie television channel

possip = positive + gossip

postel = posh + hostel

pracky = practice + hockey

Prattenegger = (Chris) Pratt + (Katherine) Schwarzenegger
prequel = pre / precede (before) + sequel
PreserVision = preserve + vision
prissy = prim + sissy
privia = privy (toilet) + trivia
pro-am = professional + amateur
prod = poke + rod
promposal = prom + proposal
pseudocide = pseudo (Greek for false) + suicide: a faked death
pubert = puberty + pervert
puggle = pug + beagle
pulsar = pulsating + star
p'zone / pizzone = pizza + calzone

Q

quarantini = quarantine + martini
quarantv = quarantine + TV
quasar = quasi (apparently, but maybe not) + stellar
quesalupa = quesadilla + chalupa (Taco Bell)

R

racino = racetrack + casino
rageaholic = rage (party) + alcoholic
Reaganomics = (Ronald) Reagan + economics
redox = reduction + oxidation
religulous = religion + ridiculous
rembarrassment = remembering + (an) embarrassment
retcon = retroactive + continuity: new but different information in
    fiction

RoboKiller = robocall + killer

rockabilly = rock + hillbilly

rockumentary = rock + documentary

Roevember = Roe (vs Wade) + November (election month)

roil = rolling / rapid + boil

Romatoes = Roma + tomatoes

romcom = romantic + comedy

rom-dram = romance + drama

rubbage = rubbish + garbage

RumChata = rum + horchata (Mexican rice drink): a cream
       liqueur

Rutube = Russian + Youtube

S

sadjectives = sad + adjectives (a Jeopardy! category)

SantaCon = Santa + convention: a global pub crawl in which adults
       dress up as Santa Claus

satisfice = satisfy + suffice

satphone = satellite + phone

scanxiety = scan + anxiety: fear of cancer after a scan

ScarJo = Scarlett + Johansson

Scarjost = Scarlett (Johansson) + (Colin) Jost; also CoJo; see
       Josthansson

schnoodle = (miniature) schnauzer + poodle

Schwatt = (Katherine) Schwarzenegger + (Chris) Pratt

sci-fi = science + fiction

scrawl = scribble + sprawl

screenager = screen + teenager: one knowledgeable about
       computers who spends a lot of time on the internet

screwvenir = screw + souvenir: when you steal something from
    someone after you slept with them

scrotch = scratch + crotch

scrunch = squeeze + crunch

scuzz = scum + fuzz

seascape = sea + landscape

SEATAC = Seattle (Washington) + Tacoma (Washington):
    International Airport

sensercize = sense + exercise (for the brain)

sexercise = sex + exercise

sexpectation = sex + expectation

sexpert = sex + expert

sext = sex + text

sextortion = sex + extortion

shacket = shirt + jacket

sharrows = shared + arrows: road markings to show a shared lane
    for cars and bicycles

shecession = she + recession: more women affected by Covid,
    inflation, etc.

SheEO = she + CEO (Chief Executive Officer)

sheepadoodle = Old English sheepdog + poodle

sheeple = sheep + people: you avoid thinking and just follow orders

Shefani = (Blake) Shelton + (Gwen) Stefani

shepherd = sheep + herder

shero = she + hero

Shih-Poo = Shih Tzu + (toy) poodle

shootie = shoe + bootie

shopaholic = shop + alcoholic

shoppertainment = shopper + entertainment

showmance = (reality) show + romance

shrinkflation = shrink + inflation: items shrink in size while prices
    go up

silk   soy + milk

Silverado = silver + El Dorado

sima = silicon + magnesium

simulcast = simultaneous + broadcast

sitcom = situation + comedy

situationship = situation + relationship: a romantic one that is
    undefined

skankles = skinny + ankles

skeezy = skeevy (unpleasant) + sleazy

skort = skirt + shorts

skullet = skull + mullet: bald on top and long hair in back

skyjack = sky + hijack

Skylab = sky + laboratory

Skype = sky + peer-to-peer

slacktivist = slacker + activist: you try to do good but don't actually
    get up out of your chair

slang = slovenly + language

slanguage = slang + language

slather = slap + lather

slawsa = slaw + salsa

slithy = lithe + slimy (appeared in Lewis Carroll's nonsense poem
    "Jabberwocky")

slofie = slow-motion + selfie

slomo = slow + motion

slop = slap + on

slurve = slider + curve: a baseball pitch

smad = sad + mad (from "The Gilmore Girls")

smash = smack + mash

smaze = smoke + haze

smedium = small + medium

smeyes / smize = smile/smiling + eyes: first coined by Tyra Banks

smishing = SMS (Short Message Service) + phishing

smog = smoke + fog

snaccident = snack + accident: eating questionable food

Snapple = snappy + apple

snark = snide + remark

snazzy = snappy + jazzy

Sneakerella = sneaker + Cinderella: a movie

snonado = snow + tornado

soca = soul + calypso

Socktober = socks + October: a charity event

SoDak = South + Dakota

SoFi = social + finance

SoHo = south (of) + Houston (Street), NYC

soundscape = sound + landscape

soylent = soybeans + lentils

Spam = spiced + ham

spanger = spare change + beggar

Spanglish = Spanish + English

spife = spoon + knife

splatter = splash + spatter

splurge = splash + surge

spoodle = (cocker) spaniel + poodle

spooktacular = spooky + spectacular

spork = spoon + fork

sporking = spooning + forking (slang for f---ing) [you're spooning
        someone and you have an erection]

sportscast = sports + broadcast

spy-fi = spy + fiction

squander = scatter + wander

squiggle = squirm + wiggle / wriggle

stagflation = stagnation + inflation: high inflation with high
    unemployment and stagnant demand

stan = stalker + fan

starchitect = star + architect

stash = store / stow + cache

staycation = stay (at home) + vacation

Steagles = (Pittsburgh) Steelers + (Philadelphia) Eagles

steez = style + ease

stormquake = storm (hurricane) + earthquake

stoup = stew + soup

streetball = street + basketball

strimmer = string + trimmer

stuber = stupid + uber

Svengeance = Sven + vengeance (from the movie *Despicable Me*)

swacked = swag + jacked (stolen)

swallop = swill + dollop (like school cafeteria food)

Swatch = Swiss + watch

swipe = sweep + wipe

swoose = swan + goose

swop = swing + hip hop

synthpop = synthesizer + popular (pop music)

Sysco = systems + services + company

T

Taebo = taekwondo + boxing

Tamiami = Tampa + Miami: the Florida road connecting them

Tampax = tampon + packs

tangelo = tangerine + pomelo: hybrid

tankini = tank (top) + bikini (bottom)

Tanzania = Tanganyika + Zanzibar: a country in East Africa

taxicab = taximeter + cabriolet

taxiety = tax + anxiety

technicolor = technical / technology + color

telecom = telephone + communication

telecommuter = telecommunications + commuter: one who works
        from home usually, also called teleworker

telegenic = television + photogenic

telehealth = telecommunication / television + health

telemedicine = telecommunication / television + medicine (more
        remote)

telethon = telephone + marathon

teletoon = television + cartoon

televangelist = television + evangelist

testomer = test + customer

testosterone = testis + sterol + ketone

Texaco = Texas + Company

Texarkana = Texas + Arkansas + Louisiana

Texican = Texan + Mexican

Texoma = Texas + Oklahoma

threenager = three-year-old + teenager: a three-year-old acting
        like a spoiled teenager

threepeat = three + repeat

throuple = three + couple (in a relationship)

tigion = tiger + lion

Tiguan = tiger + leguan (iguana): a VW car

tofurky = tofu + turkey: faux turkey usually made from tofu

Tomkat = Tom (Cruise) + Katie (Holmes)

toonie = two (dollar coin) + loonie (Canada's one-dollar coin)

tope = totally + dope

totchos = (tater) tots + nachos

tradfest = traditional + festival

tragicomedy = tragedy + comedy

Trans Am = trans (Latin for across) + America

Transformania = transform + mania: a movie

transistor = transfer + resistor

transponder = transmitter + responder

transportainment = transportation + entertainment: parties with
          music and drinking who ride or pedal slowly in large open-
          air vehicles

travelogue = travel + monologue

treeson = tree + arson

trill = true + real (slang)

Trimates = three + primates (Jane Goodall, Dian Fossey, and
          Biruté Galdikas, who studied chimpanzees, gorillas, and
          orangutans, respectively)

tripledemic = triple + epidemic (Covid, RSV, flu)

turducken = turkey + duck + chicken

tween = teen + between (ages 8-12)

twiddle = twist + fiddle

twindemic = twin + pandemic (flu and coronavirus)

twinight = twilight + night: baseball double-header

twirl = twist + whirl

twix = twin + sticks

U

ughstipated = ugh + constipated

ugleauty = ugly + beauty: feelings about yourself with which to
        come to terms

urbex = urban + exploration (illegally)

urinalysis = urine + analysis

V

vaccication = vaccination + vacation

V chip = violence + chip (to protect children)

veganuary = vegan + January

Venmo = VENdere (Latin for "to sell") + MObile

Verizon = veritas (Latin for truth) + horizon

Viacom = video + audio + communications

vidiot = video + idiot

vitameatavegamin = vitamins + meat + vegetables + minerals
      (from the "I Love Lucy" TV show)

Vlandon = Vladimir (Putin) + (Let's go) Brandon

vlog = video + log / blog

vog = volcanic + smog

voost = vitamin + boost

W

waho = Waffle + House

Wahlburgers = Wahlburg (family) + hamburgers

wallaroo = wallaby + kangaroo

Walmart = (Sam) Walton + mart

wasband = was + husband (and still a friend, from "Judge Judy") webcast = (world wide) web + broadcast

webinar = (world wide) web + seminar: meeting on the internet

webisode = web + episode

wefie (pronounced WEE-fee) = we + selfie: a group selfie

wholphin = (killer) whale + dolphin

whoodle = Wheaton terrier + poodle

WiFi = wireless + fidelity

wigger = white + n____

Wikipedia = wiki (Hawaiian for fast) + encyclopedia

Wiktionary = Wiki + dictionary

(Roger) Wilco = will + comply

workaholic = work + alcoholic

worship = worth + ship (similar to friendship; you are worthy)

Y

yakow = yak + cow

yardigras = yard + Mardi Gras (due to Covid)

yattle = yak + cattle

Yelp = yellow (pages) + help

Yoranian = Yorkshire (terrier) + Pomeranian (also called porkie)

Yorkipoo = Yorkshire terrier + (toy) poodle

yourgage = you + mortgage: a custom loan other than 15 or 30
        years

youthquake = youth + earthquake: norm shift

yummilicious = yummy + delicious

Z

zaddy = z (for emphasis) + daddy: attractive, fashionable man, first
        used in a song by Ty Dolla $ign

zalad = Zaxby's (Restaurant) + salad

Zanessa = Zak (Efron) + Vanessa (Hudgens)

zeboo = zebra + kangaroo

zedonk = zebra + donkey

Zeize = seize + Zyrtec (allergy medicine)

Zicam = zinc + ICAM-1

zonkey = zebra + donkey

zoodles = zucchini + noodles

Zoombies = zoo + zombies

zorse = zebra + horse

zumping = Zoom + dumping: breaking up

WHAT'S IN A NAME?

NAMES FROM OCCUPATIONS

When I found out my last name Smith was the most common surname (last name) in the English language and that it came from the fact that at least one of my ancestors was a blacksmith (Smith is obviously a shortened form of blacksmith), I found that very interesting and started thinking about other names and researching them. Furthermore, in the Middle Ages, if your name was John and you were a blacksmith, for example, you would be known as John the smith. Eventually it became the actual last name Smith. By the way, in Germany, it is Schmidt. In Italy, it is Ferraro, from "ferro," Italian for "iron."

Here is a list of names that come from occupations:

A

Abbot: high-ranking official in a monastery
Alderman: At first this was an Anglo-Saxon government official.
Now an alderman is a member of a municipal council.
Archer: a hunter/fighter with a bow and arrow
Armor/Armer: one who makes arms or armor
Arrowsmith: a maker of arrows, especially shafts and points

B

Bachman (German): "brook man," a ferry operator

Becker (German, corrupted from Bäcker): one who bakes

Bailey: corruption of bailiff, an officer of a municipal court

Baker: a maker of bread and cakes

Barber: a cutter of men's hair

Barker: a tanner of animal hides or a shepherd

Barns/Barnes: one having anything to do with barns

Bauer (German): a farmer

Baxter: originally meaning Baker; Bakstere is the feminine
        counterpart

Bell: a bell ringer or bell maker

Benner (German and English): either a bean farmer/seller or a
        basketmaker

Bishop: a Protestant church official

Black: a cloth dyer

Boner: one who works with bones

Booker (or German Bücher): one who works with books

Bowman (German Baumann): an archer

Braver/Braverman (German): a courageous man, a brave man

Brewer/Brewster (male/female counterparts): a brewer of beer
        and ale

Butcher: meat cutter/seller

Butler: one who assisted an upper-class person

C

Carpenter: a worker with wood

Carter: one who carries/delivers things in a cart

Cartwright: one who makes or repairs carts/wagons

Carver: one who carves

Chamberlain: servant to a nobleman who also cleaned the chambers, or rooms

Chancellor: originally a nobleman's secretary, now a government or academic official

Chandler: a candlemaker or one who deals with supplies for ships such as tar and ropes

Clark/Clarke (Old English): clerk

Cohen (from Hebrew kohen): a priest

Coleman: a coal miner

Collier: a worker with coal or charcoal

Cook/Cooke: one who cooks

Cooper: a barrel-maker

Coward: a cow herder

Cox: a helmsman or coxswain on a ship

Crocker: a potter

Currier: a finisher of leather for gloves or leather-backed books, for example

Cutler: a knife-maker

D

Digger: one who digs

Draper (from Old French "drap," which means "cloth"): a maker/seller of woolen cloth

Driver: a driver of herds of animals

Dyer: a dyer of cloth

F

Farmer: one who farms

Faulkner: a falconer

Feldman (German): a worker in the fields

Ferry: helps people cross a body of water on a ferry

Fisher (also German Fischer): one who fishes

Fletcher: one who works with arrows, especially putting on the
        feathers, or simply an arrowmaker

Forester: one who manages a forest

Fowler: a hunter of wild birds

Fuller: one who cleans wool

G

Gardner/Gardener/Gardiner: one who works in gardens

Garner: one who works with grain in a granary

Glazier: one who works with glass

Glover: one who makes/sells gloves

Granger: a farmer

Groom/Grooms: one who takes care of horses

H

Hansard (from French "hansard," which means "sword"): a sword
        maker

Harker: one who trains hawks

Harper: one who plays a harp or makes harps

Hausman (German)/Houseman (corruption of German name):
        janitor/caretaker

Hayward: a keeper of fences

Hooper: old word for cooper, a barrel maker

Hopper: one who raises hops (for beer or ale)

Hunter: one who hunts wild game

I

Inman: an innkeeper

K

Kastner / German Casner: could be a granary owner or a cabinet
    maker

Kaufmann (German) / corrupted to Koffman or Coffman: a store
    owner

Keeler: a bargeman

Kellogg (from medieval English "kellen," to kill): literally "kill
    hog;" name for a butcher of pork

Kemp/Kempe: a wrestler or athlete, from Old English "cempa," or
    "warrior"

Key: one who is a locksmith

Kirkman (Scottish): a church man or worker in a church

Kitchener: one who works in a kitchen

L

Lardner: cupboard keeper

Leach: a doctor

Lederer (German equal for Tanner or Skinner): a worker of leather

M

Mailer: one who works with "mail," another word for "armor"

Marshall: a keeper of horses

Mason: a brick or stone worker

Mercer: a merchant, especially in textiles

Miller (German Müller/ Mueller): a mill keeper, a miller of grain

P

Painter: one who paints buildings, bridges, etc.

Palmer: a pilgrim

Parker: a park keeper or gamekeeper on the estate of a nobleman

Piper: a pipe player

Potter: a pottery maker

Porter: one who carries things for other people; also a door keeper

Prentice: an apprentice

R

Reeve/Reeves: an administrative official

Roper: one who works with rope

S

Saddler/ Sadler: one who makes saddles and other leather goods

Sawyer: one who works in a saw mill; a carpenter

Schaefer/Shafer/Shaffer (German): a sheep herder

Schmidt (German): a blacksmith

Schneider/Sneider/Snyder (German): a tailor of cloth

Shepherd/Sheppard: a sheep herder

Sherman: a shearsman

Shoemaker/German Schumacher: one who repairs and makes
    shoes; a cobbler

Skinner: one who skins animals for the fur or the hide

Skully: a scholar

Slater: one who works with slate or other roof materials

Smith: a blacksmith, or metal worker; Note: you could also be a
    goldsmith or whitesmith (worker in tin); also Smythe

Steward: a warden, game keeper, manager or overseer

Stone: a worker in stone

T

Tailor/Taylor: a clothing maker

Tanner: one who dresses animal hides

Thatcher: a roofer who uses straw, etc.

Tillman/Tyler: a roof tiler

Travers/Travis: a collector on a toll bridge

Tucker: a fabric worker

Turner: one who operates a lathe, a machine that rotates so that
    operations like cutting, sanding, drilling, etc., may be
    performed

W

Wagoner/Waggoner: a wagon driver, or teamster

Wainwright/Wayne: Wainwright/Wayne: one makes or repairs
    wagons; a wheel maker makes or repairs wagons; a wheel
    maker

Wall: a mason

Weaver: a weaver of cloth

Webber/Weber: a weaver

Webster: a weaver, "maker of webs"

Wheeler: a wheelmaker

Wheelwright: one who makes wheels

A name like Johnson (or Jones) means "John's son" or "son of John." Other examples are Jackson, Williamson, Anderson, Harrison, Jameson, Morrison, Nelson, Davidson, Ericson, and Robinson. There are many more of these. (Leif) Erikson means " the son of Erik the Red." By the way, the "son" ending in Denmark takes the form of "sen" and in Poland it is "ski." In Ireland and Scotland, "mac" means "son." Sometimes it was shortened to Mc or M'. The Irish used the O' for "grandson." So McConnell was the son of Connell, and O'Connell was Connell's grandson! In Wales the word for "son of" was "ap." It was put before a name, but the "a" was dropped. For example, the children of Howell became Powell, and the children of Richard became Pritchard. Sometimes B was used instead of P, so Owen's children became Bowen. The British Isles usually shortened "son" into just an "s." For example, the son of Richard may have become Richards. The French word for "son" is "fils." This turned into "Fitz" as in Fitzgerald or Fitzpatrick, or son of Gerald and son of Patrick.

NAMES FROM PERSONAL TRAITS

A person's physical traits have been a source of family names. If a man had a reddish face, he may have had the name of Red, Reid, or Reed in England. This becomes Rousseau in France, Rossi in Italy, Roth in Germany, and Flynn in Ireland. If a man had light coloring, he may have had the last name of White in England. This becomes

Bianco in Italy, LeBlanc in France, and Weiss in Germany. Other examples are Brown, Black, and Gold.

A man named Hardy would probably have been healthy and brave. A man named Dexter would probably have been clever and right-handed. The name Braverman speaks for itself. So does Smart, Wise, and Truman.

Size and strength have also been a source of names. Examples are Strong, Power, Little, Swift, Armstrong, Longfellow, and Small. People with body parts that stood out provided names like Head, Legge, and Foot. If a man had a similar characteristic to an animal, his name might be Fox if he was cunning, Lamb if he was gentle, or Falcon if he was powerful.

OTHER NAMES FROM PEOPLE, PLACES, AND THINGS

Invaders of England sometimes tacked their own words onto names of villages or family names. Thorp/Thorpe means "farm" or "hamlet." Sometimes it corrupted into Throp. Winthrop is an example. Wick means "village," as in Pickwick. Sometimes "wick" was put first as in Wickham. Sometimes it morphed into "wich," as in "Greenwich," a "green place."

During the Middle Ages, Europeans sometimes took their family names from physical properties of the land. Some examples are Rivers, Brook, Lake, Hill, Ash, Woods, Fields, and Stone. If your last name is Clifford, it probably means "a ford (a crossing in a body of water) at a cliff." The last name Rivera also has to do with a river. The last name Castillo has to do with a castle. The last name Montana has to do with a mountain. If your last name is London, it simply comes from London, England. Milton has to do with a mill town. Last names Churchill and York have to do with location.

Many names end in -lee, -lea, and -ley, which mean "meadow." For example, Priestley probably indicated who owned the meadow. Farley meant a distant meadow.

Germanic/Dutch names for "field" are -feld, -veld, and -velt. Roosevelt means "rose field." Blumenfeld means "flowery field." The French word for field is "champ," as in Beauchamp, "beautiful field." It became the English name Beecham.

Names that end in "by" come from a Scandinavian word for "settlement." The name "Kirby" comes from "a settlement with a church." A shortened form of "homestead," "ham" forms the last part of many family names like, Dunham, Grisham, and Haversham. An old form of "town," "ton" comes at the end of many names like Walton, Hampton, Hilton, and Washington. Other suffixes that often mean town or city are -burg, -boro, -borurgh, -bury, and -ville. For example, Greenville meant "a green village." Littleton meant "a little town." Newburgh meant "a new city."

Others were named after people with one of those suffixes added. For example, Pittsburgh is a city named after William Pitt the Elder, a British prime minister.

Asheboro, North Carolina, is named for Samuel Ashe, a governor of North Carolina. Brownsville, Texas, is named for Major Jacob Brown. Burlington, Vermont, is named for the Burling family who owned the land upon which that city in Vermont was built. Charleston, South Carolina, was named after King Charles II of England. Jacksonville, Florida, is named for Andrew Jackson, the seventh President of the United States. The internet lists thousands of these cities and how they got their names. Austin, Texas, is named for Moses Austin and his son Stephen, former Texas Secretary of State. Houston, Texas, is named for Sam Houston, former governor of Texas. Denver, Colorado, is named for James Denver, the first governor of the territory. Madison, Wisconsin, is named for James Madison, the fourth President of the United States. Lincoln, Nebraska, is named for Abraham Lincoln, the sixteenth President of the United States. Bismarck, North Dakota, is named for Otto von Bismarck, former Minister President of Prussia, a German state before Germany became unified. San Francisco is named after Saint Francis of Assisi, an Italian Catholic friar who founded the Franciscan orders. He is also the patron saint of animals and ecology. Vancouver, Canada, and Vancouver, Washington, are both named for Royal Navy Captain George Vancouver. Alexandria, Egypt, is named for Alexander the Great. St. Petersburg, Russia, is named for Tsar Peter the Great and the apostle Saint Peter.

Some surnames come from one's employer, especially a church official or nobleman. Examples are King (König or Koenig in German); Kaiser (German for "emperor"); Prince; Queen; Duke; Baron / Barron; Pope; Bishop; Priest; and Abbot.

At first Jewish families had no last name, but in the early 1800s laws were passed requiring surnames. In Germany names were chosen especially from nature or location. Examples are -stein (stone), such as Goldstein, Silverstein, and Rubenstein; -thal (valley), such as Blumenthal (flower valley) and Rosenthal (rose valley); -berg (mountain), such as Rosenberg (rose mountain) and Goldberg (gold mountain); -baum (tree), such as Mandelbaum (almond tree), Rosenbaum (rose tree), Grünbaum (green tree) and Tannenbaum (evergreen tree). Poland and Russia adopted similar systems.

Slaves brought to America from Africa had difficult first and last names so their masters gave them a name. Free slaves had to have a surname as well in order to vote. Some took the last name of their former masters or the name of the county in which they lived (which was often the name of a famous person). Some just chose a name they liked or the name of someone they respected or admired. Common ones were Jefferson, Jackson, and Washington (ironic because they owned slaves). Even more surprising is the fact that their liberator Abraham Lincoln was not a common choice.

Many first names simply come from the Bible: Matthew, Mark, Luke, John, David, Noah, Daniel, Aaron, Samuel, Gabriel, Levi, Simon, Adam, Joseph, Jesus, Michael, Thomas, Ethan, Ezra, Andrew, Nathan, Reuben, Peter, Jeremiah (hence Jeremy also), Deborah, Judith, Sarah, Naomi, Hannah, Rebecca, Esther, Rachel, Ruth, Abigail, Anna, Bernice, Mary, Elizabeth, Eve, Leah, Martha, Miriam, and many more.

Many people chose names because of their meaning, for example, Ann/Anna means "grace." Christopher means "bearer of Christ." Susanna means "lily." David means "beloved." Ethan means "enduring." Liam (short for WilLIAM) means "protector." Noah means "peace." Belinda/Linda means "beautiful." Amy means "beloved." Valerie means "valiant." Victor means "conqueror." Victoria means "victorious." Helen or Helene comes from the Greek *helios*, which means "sun." Margaret or Marguerite comes from the Greek *margarite*, which means "pearl." Deborah comes from a Hebrew word meaning "bee." Theodore comes from the Greek *Theas*, which means "God." Alice ("truth"), Phyllis ("green leaf"), Philip ("lover of horses"), and Irene ("peace") all come from the Greek language. Carol or Caroline means "strong," the female version of Charles. My name, Charlotte, also came from my father's name Charles. The preceding four names come from Latin. Justin comes from the Latin justus *for* *"just."* Other names from Latin are Gloria ("glory") and Lawrence ("crowned with laurel"). Absalom means "father of peace." Beatrice means "blessed." The list goes on and on. By the way, the Irish name for Jane is "Sinead." In Scotland Ian is the same as William. Jose is the same as Giuseppe and Joseph. In Wales Evan is the same as John. Other names for John are Juan, Ian, and Ivan.

Do you ever wonder why a "christening" is called that? In many countries a child's first name was given at baptism. It was called the child's "Christian name," which is probably a shortened form of "christening name." "Given name" applies to all religions.

Many girls are named after flowers. Examples are Lily, Rose, Daisy, and Jasmine. Your name may come from a character in a book or an artist or a musician or a writer. Your name may have a unique spelling. I named my son after a character on a soap opera whose name I liked--Brandon.

The word *nickname* comes from Old English "ekename," "eke" meaning "additional." Therefore, a nickname is an additional name. Michael becomes Mike. Abigail becomes Abby. Alexander becomes Alex. Andrew becomes Andy. Rebecca becomes Becky. Benjamin becomes Ben. Elizabeth becomes Beth or Liz or Betsy. Robert becomes Bob. Christopher becomes Chris or Topher (interesting). David becomes Dave. Francis becomes Frank. August becomes Auggie or Gus. Judith becomes Judy. Patrick becomes Pat. Peter becomes Pete. Philip or Phillip becomes Phil. Tobias becomes Toby. Victoria becomes Vicky. William becomes Will or Bill or Liam. Other common nicknames are Larry, Luke, Steve, Kate, Ken, Kathy, Nick, Tommy, Matt, Josh, Zeke, Peggy (from Margaret), Espy (from Esperanza), Joe, Sam, Sue, Jim, Rick, Jake, Fred, Dan, Greg, Ray, Rob, Ron, Ed or Eddie, and Zach. Again, the list goes on and on. On the humorous side, a thin man may be called Slim, a large person may be called Tiny, a bald man may be called Curly, or a left-handed person may be called Lefty. I have called people Smiley (for obvious reasons) and Bunny (because she had energy like the Energizer bunny). I have been called Char and even Chuck.

New Zealanders are called Kiwis and Australians are called
Aussies. One from England may be called a Limey because a long time
ago English sailors were given limes to protect them from scurvy.

MISCELLANEOUS FUN WITH NAMES

In 2016, 4,746 people had the same first and last name. Some
of the most common ones are Alexander Alexander, Rose Rose,
Thomas Thomas, Santiago Santiago, Grace Grace, Rosa Rosa, James
James, Kelly Kelly, and Ruth Ruth. Furthermore, 45,379 people had
names like John Johnson, Edward Edwards, Robert Robertson, Jens
Jensen, Martin Martinez, and William Williams. Sometimes names
included the father's name like Eva Evans or Rose Rosen/Rosenberg.

Then there are names that end with their first names. Examples
are Gerald Fitzgerald, Donald McDonald/MacDonald, and Patrick
Fitzpatrick. Many names rhyme like Mary Berry, Mark Park, Bart
Hart, and Jack Black. There are many Ronald McDonalds!

There is always an hilarious name of a town or city or
unincorporated area in every state. Let's have some fun with those.

Alabama: Scratch Ankle; Bacon Level; Blue Eye; Burnout; Burnt
        Corn; Coffee Pot; Intercourse; Normal
Alaska: Chicken; Deadhorse
Arizona: Why; Nothing; Snowflake; Darling
Arkansas: Greasy Corner; Toad Suck; Fifty-Six; Flippin;
        Smackover; Romance
California: Rough and Ready; Zzyzx; Charming
Colorado: No Name; Arriba; Dinosaur; Hygiene; Paradox; Lay
Connecticut: Satan's Kingdom; Hazardville
Delaware: Blue Ball; Slaughter Beach; Bacons

Florida: Two Egg; Christmas; Couch; Dogtown; Fluffy Landing;
    Needmore; Niceville; Picnic; Spuds

Georgia: Hopeulikit; Experiment; Climax; Between; Social Circle;
    Enigma; The Rock; Valentine

Hawaii: Papa; Nine Miles

Idaho: Slick Poo; Good Grief

Illinois: Goofy Ridge; Normal; Birds; Oblong; Muddy; Boody

Indiana: Santa Claus; Gnaw Bone; Toad Hop

Iowa: What Cheer; Defiance; Lost Nation

Kansas: Buttermilk; Smileyberg; Gas; Agenda

Kentucky: Monkey's Eyebrow; Bigbone

Louisiana: Coochie

Maine: Friendship; Mexico

Maryland: Accident; Friendsville; Secretary; Crapo; Chevy Chase;
    Fruitland

Massachusetts: Buzzards Bay; Cow Yard; Five Pound Island

Michigan: Hell; Christmas; Temperance; Paradise; Jugville

Minnesota: Climax; Nimrod; Embarrass; Sleepy Eye; Ball Club

Mississippi: Money; Alligator; Soso; Basic; Darling

Missouri: Peculiar; Tightwad; Humansville; Romance

Montana: Square Butte; Contact; Content; Cowboys Heaven;
    Stoner Place; Tobacco

Nebraska: Funk; Magnet; Surprise; Valentine

Nevada: Jackpot; Puckerbrush; Lovelock

New Hampshire: Dummer; Center Sandwich; Happy Corner; Hell
    Hollow

New Jersey: Buttzville; Quibbletown

New Mexico: Truth or Consequences; Candy Kitchen

New York: Chili; Butternuts; Horseheads; Triangle; Calcium,
    North Pole

North Carolina: Whynot; Lizard Lick; Boogertown; Toast; Climax

North Dakota: Zap; Deep; Concrete; Flasher

Ohio: Knockemstiff; Pee Pee

Oklahoma: Slaughterville; Moon; Non; IXL; Mustang

Oregon: Boring; Zigzag

Pennsylvania: Intercourse; Bird in Hand; Mars; Paint; Peach
      Bottom; Pillow; Climax; Darling

Rhode Island: Scituate

South Carolina: Ketchuptown; Fingertown; Ninety Six

South Dakota: Mud Butte; Peever; Gayville

Tennessee: Bitter End; Finger; Guys; Nutbush; Sweet Lips

Texas: Ding Dong; Nameless; Cut and Shoot; Uncertain; Jot-Em-
      Down; Cool; Blessing; Valentine; Darling; Lovelady

Utah: Escalante; Mexican Hat

Vermont: Bread Loaf; Mosquitoville; Adamant; Eden

Virginia: Fries; Assawoman; Tightsqueeze; Overall; Croaker;
      Dismal Town; Needmore; Lick Skillet; Valentines

Washington: Welcome; Medical Lake; Tokeland; Vader

West Virginia: Booger Hole; Paw Paw; Kermit; Odd; Man; Nitro;
      Hundred; Pie

Wisconsin: Embarrass; Fence; Bosstown; Disco; Luck

Wyoming: West Thumb; Recluse; Story

PALINDROMES

A palindrome can be a word, phrase, sentence, or number. It reads the same forward or backward. An example of a palindromic word is level. An example of a palindromic phrase is "a man, a plan, a canal--Panama." An example of a palindromic sentence is "Step on no pets." The last time a year was a palindrome was 2002 and before that 1991. Can you figure out the next one?

Other examples of palindromic numbers are 1441 and 555. If you take any number, reverse the digits, add the two numbers, and do this over and over, you will get a palindromic number! It could take one time or fifty or more times, but it will happen if you do not make any mistakes. So be careful when you try this. To begin with, just try a three-digit or four-digit number. Nevertheless, it works for all numbers.

Examples:

4051	863
<u>1504</u>	<u>368</u>
5555 Done!	1231
	<u>1321</u>
	1552
	<u>2551</u>

4103
<u>3014</u>
7117 Done!

Palindrome Days occur when the date can be read the same backward and forward. Examples are 11-11-11, 2-22-22, and 02-02-2020. People love to get married on these types of dates!

The above palindromes are called reciprocal. They all read exactly the same backwards and forwards. By the way, recurrent palindromes are different words when read backwards and forwards. They are also called back words or reverse pairs. Examples are stop and pots, rat and tar, and loop and pool. Even more interesting is the fact that such a word is also called a Levidrome. In 2017 a second-grader from Canada named Levi Budd thought there was no word for this situation and coined the word Levidrome. However, there is a word for this, and it cracks me up! In 1961 Martin Gardner and C. C. Bombaugh came up with "semordnilap," which is "palindromes" spelled backwards! It would have been better if it were singular, in my opinion. Other examples are stressed and desserts, reward and drawer, God and dog, saw and was, raw and war, mug and gum, live and evil, keep and peek, rail and liar, stops and spots, laced and decal, sleep and peels, sleek and keels, snips and spins, ram and mar, tips and spit, bats and stab, rats and star, devil and lived, trams and smart, warts and straw, deliver and reviled, and diaper and repaid. How fun!

Some palindromes are word units. That is, the order of the words is the same backward and forward. Here is an example by James Albert Lindon, a British poet and word expert: You can cage a swallow, can't you, but you can't swallow a cage, can you? Here is another one: Eat to live, never live to eat.

SOME PALINDROMIC WORDS

ABBA, the famous Swedish band

Ada

aibohphobia (fear of palindromes!)

Ana

Anna

Ava

bib

Bob

boob

bub

civic

dad

deed

deified

dewed

did

dud

Elle

ere

Eve

ewe

eye

gag

gig

hah

halah

Hannah

Harrah

huh

kayak

kook

lemel (leftover precious metal dust after shaping)

level

Lil

ma'am

minim (1/60 of a dram, about a drop of liquid)

mom

mum

murdrum (killing someone unknown)

naan (a South Asian bread)

Nan

noon

nun

Otto

pap

peep

pep

pip

poop

pop

pup

radar

redder

redivider

refer

repaper

reviver

rotator

rotavator (a type of machine that breaks up soil)

rotor

sagas

sexes

sis

solos

SOS

stats

tat

tit

Tebet/Tevet (tenth month of the Jewish religious year)

tenet

toot

tot

tut

wow

xanax

yay

SOME TWO-WORD PALINDROMES

avid diva

Dr. Awkward

emu fume

liar trail

llama mall

my gym

Noose? Soon.

not on

porch crop

pot top

race car

red-ice cider

sewer ewes

smart trams

stiff fits

Tahiti hat

top spot

SOME PALINDROMIC PHRASES

An error, Rena

An igloo pool, Gina

A man, a plan, a canal--Panama

A Santa at NASA

Borrow or rob?

Campus motto: bottoms up, Mac

Dad's dad's dad

Mad at Adam?

Massive Levis, Sam

murder for a jar of red rum

never odd or even

No dresser, Don?

no melons, no lemon

no trace; not one carton

Oh, no, Don Ho

remarkable Melba Kramer

so many dynamos

taco cat

SOME PALINDROMIC SENTENCES

Able was I ere I saw Elba.

Dennis sinned.

Doc, note I dissent. A fast never prevents a fatness. I diet on cod.

Don't nod.

Draw, O Coward!

Eva, can I stab bats in a cave?

Flo, gin is a sin. I golf.

Live not on evil.

Madam, I'm Adam.

Madam, in Eden, I'm Adam.

Mr. Owl ate my metal worm.

Nate bit a Tibetan.

Ron, I'm a minor.

Step on no pets.

'Tis Ivan on a visit.

Too bad I hid a boot.

Was it a can on a cat I saw?

Was it a car or a cat I saw?

Was it a rat I saw?

Won't I panic in a pit now?

Won't lovers revolt now?

INTERESTING PLURALS

Note: If a plural ends in -ae, it is pronounced like long e unless otherwise noted. If a plural ends in i, it is a long i unless otherwise noted.

SINGULAR	PLURAL
A	
A	As
abacus	abacuses / abaci
acropolis	acropolises
actum	acta
addendum	addenda / addendums
agora	agoras / agorae
aircraft	aircraft
alga	algae / algas
alluvium	alluvia
alto	altos
alumna (F)	alumnae
alumnus (M)	alumni
amoeba	amoebas / amoebae
analysis	analyses

anime	anime / animes
antenna	antennae / antennas
antithesis	antitheses
antrum	antra
aorta	aortas / aortae
apex	apexes / apices
appendix	appendices / appendixes
aquarium	aquariums / aquaria
arboretum	arboretums / arboreta
asylum	asyla / asylums
attorney general	attorneys general
atrium	atriums / atria
auditorium	auditoriums / auditoria
aura	auras / aurae
ax	axes (tools)
axis	axes (coordinate planes)

B

baby	babies
bacillus	bacilli
bacterium	bacteria
banjo	banjos / banjoes
basis	bases
bass (fish)	bass / basses
bass (singer)	basses / bass
beau	beaus / beaux
beef	beefs / beeves

belief	beliefs
berry	berries
biceps	biceps / bicepses
bison	bison
box	boxes
boy	boys
brother-in-law	brothers-in-law
buffalo	buffalo / buffalos / buffaloes
bureau	bureaus / bureaux
Burns	Burnses
bus	buses

C

cactus	cacti / cactuses
cafeteria	cafeterias
calamara (F) / calamoro (M)	calamari
calf	calves / calfs
candelabrum	candelabra / candelabrums
cargo	cargoes
carpel (part of a flower)	carpels
carpus (wristbone)	carpi
cello	cellos / celli (i sounds like long e)
cerebellum	cerebellums / cerebella
chateau	chateaux / chateaus
cherub	cherubim / cherubs
chief	chiefs
child	children

chimney	chimneys
Chinese	Chinese
cilium	cilia
cirrus	cirri
coccyx (tailbone)	coccyxes / coccyges
cod	cod
codex	codexes / codices
colon	colons / cola
colossus	colossi
company	companies
compendium	compendia / compendiums
concerto	concertos / concerti (i sounds like long e)
condominium	condominiums / condominia
confetto	confetti
consortium	consortia / consortiums
copy	copies
corona	coronas / coronae
corps	corps
corpus	corpora
counsel	counsel
country	countries
coxa (hipbone)	coxae
cranium	crania / craniums
crematorium	crematoriums / crematoria
crisis	crises
criterion	criteria / criterions
cry	cries
cul-de-sac	culs-de-sac / cul-de-sacs

cumulus	cumuli
cupful	cupfuls
curriculum	curriculums / curricula

D

daisy	daisies
datum	data
daughter-in-law	daughters-in-law
deer	deer
delirium	deliriums / deliria
diagnosis	diagnoses
dictionary	dictionaries
dictum	dicta / dictums
die	dice
discus	discuses
domino	dominoes / dominos
donkey	donkeys
duo	duos
dwarf	dwarfs / dwarves

E

echo	echoes
ego	egos
elf	elves
elk	elk
ellipsis	ellipses
embargo	embargoes / embargos

embryo	embryos
emphasis	emphases
emporium	emporia / emporiums
ephemeron	ephemera
equilibrium	equilibria / equilibriums
erratum	errata
essay	essays
Eskimo	Eskimos / Eskimo
eyelash	eyelashes

F

family	families
father-in-law	fathers-in-law
fauna	faunae / faunas
femur (thighbone)	femurs / femora
fibula (calf bone)	fibulas / fibulae
fireman	firemen
fish	fish / fishes
flagellum	flagella
flora	florae / floras
fly	flies
focus	foci / focuses
foot	feet
formula	formulas / formulae
forum	forums / fora
fowl	fowl
fox	foxes

fresco	frescoes / frescos
fungus	fungi / funguses

G

gelato	gelatos / gelati (i sounds like long e)
genesis	geneses
genie	genies / genii
genius	geniuses / genii
genus	genera / genuses
geranium	geraniums / gerania
gladiolus	gladioli / gladioluses
gluteus	glutei / gluteuses
goose	geese
graffito	graffiti (i sounds like long e)
grandchild	grandchildren
grapefruit	grapefruit / grapefruits
grouse	grouse
gymnasium	gymnasia / gymnasiums

H

half	halves
handful	handfuls
handkerchief	handkerchiefs
harmonium	harmoniums
helix	helices
hero	heroes

herring	herring
hippopotamus	hippopotamuses / hippopotami
hobo	hobos / hobos
hoof	hooves / hoofs
hovercraft	hovercraft / hovercrafts
hypothesis	hypotheses

I

iamb	iambi / iambs
igloo	igloos
ignoramus	ignoramuses
ilium (pelvic bone)	ilia
illiteratus	illiterati (ending i sounds like long e)
incubus	incubi / incubuses
index	indices / indexes
innuendo	innuendoes / innuendos

J

Jones	Joneses
journey	journeys

K

kangaroo	kangaroos
key	keys

knife	knives
kudos	kudos

L

labellum	labella / labellums
labium	labia
lacuna (a gap)	lacunae
lady	ladies
larva	larvae / larvas
lasagna	lasagne
leaf	leaves
library	libraries
libretto	libretti (ending i sounds like long e) / librettos
life	lives
literatus	literati (ending i sounds like long e)
lithium	lithia / lithiums
loaf	loaves
locus	loci
louse	lice

M

magnesium	magnesia / magnesiums
magnum	magna / magnums
magus	magi
man	men

manifesto	manifestoes / manifestos
matrix	matrices / matrixes
maximum	maxima / maximums
medium	media / mediums
medulla	medullae / medullas
memento	mementos / mementoes
memo	memos
memorandum	memoranda / memorandums
meninx (skull membrane)	meninges
merry-go-round	merry-go-rounds
metamorphosis	metamorphoses
metastasis	metastases
millenium	millenia / milleniums
minimum	minima / minimums
minutia	minutiae
modem	modems
memento	mementos / mementoes
momentum	momenta / momentums
mongoose	mongooses
monkey	monkeys
moose	moose
moratorium	moratoria / moratoriums
mosquito	mosquitoes / mosquitos
mother-in-law	mothers-in-law
motto	mottoes / mottos
mouse	mice
mulatto	mulattoes / mulattos

N

nautilus	nautiluses / nautili
nebula	nebulae / nebulas
necropolis	necropolises / necropoles / necropoleis / necropoli
nemesis	nemeses
neurosis	neuroses
nexus	nexus / nexuses
nimbus	nimbi (ending i sounds like long e) / nimbuses
9	9s
1990	1990s
no	noes
notum	nota
nova	novas / novae
nucleus	nuclei / nucleuses

O

oasis	oases
octopus	octopuses / octopi
oculus	oculi (i sounds like long e)
odeon / odeum	odea
offspring	offspring
operandus	operandi (i sounds like long e)
opium	opiums / opia
optimum	optima / optimums

opus	opera
ourself	ourselves
ovum	ova
ox	oxen

P

pandemonium	pandemonia / pandemoniums
panino	panini
paparazzo	paparazzi (i sounds like long e)
papilla	papillae
parenthesis	parentheses
passer-by	passers-by
patio	patios
penny	pennies / pence
people	people / peoples
perch (n. a fish)	perch
person	persons / people
phalanx	phalanges
phenomenon	phenomena / phenomenons
phylum	phyla
piano	pianos
pike	pike
pizza	pizzas / pizze
planetarium	planetariums / planetaria
plateau	plateaus / plateaux
pliers	pliers
podium	podiums / podia

policeman	policemen
polyhedron	polyhedra / polyhedrons
pony	ponies
portfolio	portfolios
potato	potatoes
prefix	prefixes
premise	premises
premises	premises
premium	premiums
president-elect	presidents-elect
prognosis	prognoses
proof	proofs
proscenium (part of stage in front of curtain)	proscenia
psychosis	psychoses
pupa	pupas / pupae

Q

quantum	quanta
quiz	quizzes
quorum	quora / quorums

R

radio	radios
radium	radiums
radius	radii / radiuses

ratio	ratios
rebus	rebuses
referendum	referenda / referendums
reindeer	reindeer
rhinoceros	rhinoceros / rhinoceroses
rodeo	rodeos
roof	roofs
rostrum	rostra / rostrums
rotunda	rotundas
runner-up	runners-up

S

sacrum (a lower back bone)	sacra
salmon	salmon
sanitarian	sanitarians
sanitarium	sanitariums / sanitaria
sanitorium	sanitoriums / sanatoria
sarcophagus	sarcophagi / sarcophaguses
scapula (shoulder blade)	scapulas / scapulae
scarf	scarves / scarfs
schema	schemata / schemas
scheme	schemes
scissors	scissors
secretary of state	secretaries of state
self	selves
septum	septa
seraph	seraphim
series	series

serum	sera / serums
shad	shad
shamble	shambles
shambles	shambles
sheaf	sheaves
sheep	sheep
shelf	shelves
shovelful	shovelfuls
shrimp	shrimp / shrimps
silo	silos
sister-in-law	sisters-in-law
sit-in	sit-ins
sky	skies
Smith	Smiths
sodium	sodiums
sola (pea family plant)	solae (-ae sounds like long a) / solas
solarium	solaria / solariums
solo	solos / soli (i sounds like long e)
soprano	sopranos
spacecraft	spacecraft
spaghetto	spaghetti (i sounds like long e)
species	species
spectrum	spectra / spectrums
sphinx	sphinxes / sphinges
spoonful	spoonfuls
spy	spies
squid	squid
stadium	stadia / stadiums

stasis	stases
stela (stone marker)	stelae
sternum (breastbone)	sterna / sternums
stigma	stigmata / stigmas
stimulus	stimuli / stimuluses
story	stories
stratum	strata
studio	studios
stylus	styli (i sounds like long e) / styluses
swine	swine
Swiss	Swiss
syllabus	syllabi / syllabuses
symposium	symposia / symposiums
synopsis	synopses

T

tableau	tableaus / tableaux
tablespoonful	tablespoonfuls
talus (anklebone)	tali (i sounds like long e)
tankful	tankfuls
tarsus	tarsi (i sounds like long e)
teaspoonful	teaspoonfuls
tedium	tediums / tedia
tempo	tempos / tempi (i sounds like long e)
tenor	tenors
terminus	termini

terrarium	terraria / terrariums
tessera	tesserae
testis	testes
tetra	tetras
that	those
thesaurus	thesauruses / thesauri
thesis	theses
thief	thieves
this	these
tibia (shinbone)	tibias / tibiae (pronounced like tibia)
titanium	titania / titaniums
toga	togas / togae (-ae pronounced like long a)
tomato	tomatoes
tongs	tongs
tooth	teeth
tornado	tornadoes / tornados
torpedo	torpedoes
torso	torsos / torsi (i sounds like long e)
torus (geometrical term)	toruses / tori (i sounds like long e)
toy	toys
triceps	triceps / tricepses
trivium	trivia / triviums
trout	trout
tuna	tuna
turkey	turkeys

tweezers	tweezers

U

uranium	uraniums
uterus	uteri / uteruses

V

valley	valleys
vertebrae	vertebras / vertebrae (-ae sounds like long a)
vertex	vertices / vertexes
veto	vetoes
video	videos
virtuosi	virtuosi (ending i sounds like long e) / virtuosos
viscus	viscera
vita	vitae / vitas
volcano	volcanoes / volcanos
vortex	vortices / vortexes

W

waltz	waltzes
watch	watches
watercraft	watercraft
wharf	wharves / wharfs

wife	wives
wolf	wolves
woman	women

Y

yourself	yourselves

Z

zero	zeroes / zeros
zirconium	zirconia / zirconiums
zoo	zoos

CONTRACTIONS

A contraction is made by putting together two or more words with certain letters left out. An apostrophe (') is used in place of the missing letters. It is best not to use them in formal writing. The following are contractions used in the English language:

CONTRACTION	MEANING
aren't	are not
can't	cannot
couldn't	could not
couldn't've (informal)	could not have
could've	could have
didn't	did not
doesn't	does not
don't	do not
e'er (literary)	ever
hadn't	had not
hasn't	has not
haven't	have not
he'd	he had / he would
he'll	he will / he shall

here's	here is
he's	he is / he has
how's	how is / how does / how has
how've	how have
I'd	I had / I should / I would
I'll	I will / I shall
I'm	I am
isn't	is not
it'd	it had / it would
it'll	it will / it shall
it's	it is
I've	I have
let's	let us
mightn't	might not
might've	might have
mustn't	must not
must've	must have
'neath (literary)	beneath
needn't	need not
ne'er (literary)	never
o'clock	of the clock
o'er (literary)	over
she'd	she had / she would
she'll	she will / she shall
she's	she is
shouldn't	should not
should've	should have
shouldn't've (informal)	should not have
tain't	it ain't (nonstandard)

that'll	that will / that shall
that's	that is
there'd	there had / there would
there'll	there will / there shall
there're	there are
there's	there is
they'll	they will / they shall
they're	they are
they've	they have
this'll	this will / this shall
'til (literary)	until
'tis (literary)	it is
'twas (literary)	it was
'twill (literary)	it will
'twixt (between, literary)	betwixt
wasn't	was not
we'd	we had / we should / we would
we'll	we will / we shall
we're	we are
weren't	were not
we've	we have
what'd	what did / what had / what would
what'll	what will / what shall
what's	what is
where's	where is
who'd	who had / who would
who'll	who will / who shall
who's	who is / who has

who've	who have
won't	will not
wouldn't	would not
would've	would have
y'all	you all
you'd	you had / you would
you'll	you will / you shall
you're	you are

BRAND NAMES AND GENERICIDE

genericide (n.) the process by which a brand name
loses it unique identity due to its popularity and is now
being used to refer to any like product or service

Many brand names turn into generic words (words relating to a group of things and not specific words). A majority of the people refer to the following items as if they were generic and not brand names, and they think nothing of it. These brands must be very special in order for this to happen, and they are.

1. Kleenex: For the majority of people, this is their go-to "tissue."
2. Crock-Pot: Invented in 1940 and used by the majority of people, the Crock-Pot brand name is used to describe any type of "slow cooker."
3. Tupperware: In 1948 a housewife named Brownie Wise from Detroit, Michigan, had the first Tupperware party. It is still a billion-dollar business. Now we refer to any "plastic container" as Tupperware.
4. Hula Hoop: Even though these types of hoops have been around a very long time, when the Hula Hoop was patented in 1964 by Wham-O it was the best. It has made a comeback these days, and now any "toy hoop" is called a Hula Hoop.

5. Band-Aid: Johnson & Johnson patented the brand in 1920. Millions are sold every year in the United States alone. When we need a "bandage," we ask for a Band-Aid.

6. Chapstick: In the 1800s a pharmacist from Lynchburg, Virginia, named Charles Browne Fleet invented Chapstick. It was not popular then, but now we spend millions and millions of dollars on Chapstick. It is no wonder that the word Chapstick is used instead of "lip balm."

7. Ziploc: The Ziploc brand is worth billions of dollars. Different stories appear about who invented it. Dow Chemical Company marketed it in 1968, but now SC Johnson makes them. We just call all those "plastic bags" Ziplocs.

8. Xerox: The Xerox Company hated that their brand name was genericized. It was one of the first. We do not say "copy." We just say Xerox whether we use it as a noun or verb.

9. Post-it: In 1974 Arthur Fry, a scientist at 3M, came up with the idea. Around 1980 Post-its hit the market. At least fifty billion are made every year. We just say "I need a Post-it" instead of "sticky note."

10. Jacuzzi: Jacuzzi is a brand name of "hot tub." We are just as apt to say "Let's get in the Jacuzzi" as often as "Let's get in the hot tub" even though the hot tub you are getting into is not even a Jacuzzi!

11. Saran Wrap: Dow originally introduced it in 1949, but now SC Johnson owns the brand name. The words Saran Wrap have come to be used for any "plastic cling wrap" in the kitchen.

12. Wite-Out: Bic makes Wite-Out, and it is the number one "correction fluid." We ALWAYS say Wite-Out!

13. Q-Tip: Q stands for quality, and they're not kidding. Everyone says Q-Tip, not "ear swab."

14. Velcro: In 1941 George de Mestral, a Swiss engineer, was walking in the woods with his dog. Burrs attached themselves to his pants and his dog's fur. For fourteen years he perfected his idea of a "hook-and-loop fastener." In 1955 his idea came to light. Now we just say Velcro for these "sticky fabric strips."

15. Aspirin: Aspirin is a specific brand of painkiller that was invented by Bayer in 1915. Bayer no longer owns the trademark. Today we call all these types of painkillers just aspirin.

16. Popsicle: In 1905 Frank Epperson was an eleven year-old boy in Oakland, California. He accidentally left his soda with a stirring stick in it outside during a very cold night. It froze, and the rest is history. He called it Epsicle, but later his own children called it Pop's sicle which obviously morphed into Popsicle. It was patented in 1955. We don't ask for a "frozen treat on a stick." We ask for a Popsicle.

17. Frisbee: Around 1920 Yale students would throw pie plates around for fun. They would yell "Frisbie!" just like golfers yell "Fore!" Frisbee is now a brand name, and nearly countless ones are sold every year. The word Frisbee now describes any "flying disc."

18. Thermos: Thermos has come to mean any "vacuum insulation" to keep things hot. The word "thermos" is Greek for "hot," coined in the early 1900s.

19. Onesie: Adults, not only babies, are wearing Onesies these days. Gerber makes the baby Onesie, but even if you own one by another company, you will call it a onesie, not a "one-piece garment."

20. Jell-O: Jell-O goes all the way back to 1897, so it's no wonder we call any "gelatin dessert" just Jell-O.

21. Sharpie: We love our Sharpies, invented in 1964. We usually do not say "permanent marker." We just call them Sharpies.

22. Dumpster: Dumpster is a brand name. In the early 30s in Knoxville, Tennessee, George Dempster and his brothers owned a construction business. They invented the Dempster-Dumpster that could be emptied mechanically into a garbage truck. The Dumpster brand name arose out of the portmanteau ("port-man-toe") of Dump + Dempster. It was patented in 1935. Now we just say dumpster instead of "waste container."

23. Bubble Wrap: There are other generic versions of this "cushioning device for shipping or packing." Nevertheless we just call it all bubble wrap. It was invented in 1957 by engineers Alfred Fielding and Marc Chavannes from Hawthorne, New Jersey.

24. Playbill: Originally, Playbill was the name of a magazine that, in 1884, was printed for one theater in New York City. Now we always get playbills instead of "programs" when we go to a play.

25. Zamboni: In 1949 Frank Zamboni invented the first ice-surfacing machine. Therefore the Zamboni is called an eponym because it was named after Frank Zamboni. These days all of these types of machines are just called zambonis even though Zamboni is a brand name.

Brand names Google and Photoshop have become verbs! Google is THE search engine! Furthermore, we just say photoshop instead of "edit the picture." Zoom is on the road to genericide. As many people or more call a table tennis table a ping-pong table even though

Ping-Pong is a brand name. Taser is a brand name and an acronym for Thomas A. Swift's Electric Rifle, invented in the 1970s by Jack Cover and inspired by a book he read. The word taser has come to be used for any "electric shock weapon or stun gun." Lava Lamp is a brand name that has been genericized. Rollerblades is a brand name invented by two hockey-playing brothers in 1980. Again the name has been genericized. Due to Covid, the word plexiglass is a household word. However, it is a brand name. But who wants to say "sneeze guard" or "acrylic shield?" Koozie is a brand name, but we have taken that capital K off and put those koozies around our drinks to keep them cold.

BIBLIOGRAPHY

Alabama. www.al.com/

Ancestry. www.ancestry.com/

Archive. www.archive.nytimes.com/

Bobber. www.bobber.discoverWisconsin.com/

Carroll, Lewis. 2012. "Jabberwocky." In *The Norton Anthology of World Literature, 1219-1220. New York, New York: W. W. Norton & Company.*

Dictionary. www.dictionary.com/

ECS Learning Systems. 1992. San Antonio, Texas: Asteria Education.

English Hints. www.englishhints.com/

English Study Online. englishstudyonline.com/

Fisher, Ken. "Super Quiz." The Santa Fe New Mexican, 2021-2022.

Grammar Party. www.grammarpartyblog.com/

Hongkiat. www.hongkiat.com/

Iheart. www.iheart.com/

Jeopardy. 2021-2022. On CBS.

Jerseys Best. www.jerseysbest.com/

Judge Judy. 2021-2022. On NBC.

Kearney Hub. www.kearneyhub.com/

Let's Run. www.let'srun.com/

Madison. www.madison.com/

Mass Realty. www.massrealty.com/

Mental Floss. www.mentalfloss.com/

Merriam-Webster's Collegiate Dictionary. 11th ed. Springfield, MA:
        Merriam-Webster Incorporated. 2003.

Merriam-Webster. www.merriam-webster.com.2021-2022./

Newstalk KGVO. www.newstalkkgvo.com/

Only in Your State. www.onlyinyourstate.com/

Oxford Languages. www.oxfordlanguages.com/

Popsicle. www.popsicle.com/

Quality Logo Products. www.qualitylogoproducts.com/

Santa Fe NEW Mexican Super Quiz. 2021-2023.

Select Surnames. www.selectsurnames.com/

Sightword Games. www.sightwordgames.com/

The Bathroom Entertainment Book. Saddle River, NJ: Red-Letter Press.
        1988.

The Today Show. February 17, 2020. On NBC.

Thinking Worship. www.thinkingworship.com/

Twitter. www.mobile.twitter.com/

Urban Dictionary. www.urbandictionary.com/

Vappingo. www.vappingo.com/

Visit Florida. www.visitflorida.com/

Wikipedia. www.en.m.wikipedia.org/

Wordpress. www.wordpress.com/

Your Dictionary. www.yourdictionary.com/

ABOUT THE AUTHOR

Charlotte Smith is a retired teacher of high school mathematics, English, and library science. She has a BS in math and an MEd. Originally from Memphis, Tennessee, she has lived in Santa Fe, New Mexico, since 2005. She uses a casual writing style with a sense of humor and an intent to educate whenever possible. Most of her books have been written to help English as a Second Language learners. They include Homophones: Words That Sound Alike; Confusing Words, Including Heteronyms; Homonyms: Multiple-Meaning Words; a children's picture book entitled Billy the Bully Goat Learns a Lesson. Future books include Compound Words and Roots and Affixes.

Printed in the United States
by Baker & Taylor Publisher Services